This book belongs to

OXFORD

UNIVERSITY PRESS

Great Clarendon Street, Oxford, OX2 6DP, United Kingdom

Oxford University Press is a department of the University
of Oxford. It furthers the University's objective of excellence
in research, scholarship, and education by publishing worldwide.
Oxford is a registered trade mark of Oxford University Press
in the UK and in certain other countries

Sam's Backpack
Text © Teresa Heapy 2017
Illustrations © Sarah Horne 2017

Bam and Red
Text © Michelle Robinson 2017
Illustrations © Ashley King 2017

A Bump in the Bed
Text © Narinder Dhami 2017
Illustrations © Feronia Parker-Thomas 2017

The Dragon Balloon
Text © Cheryl Palin 2017
Illustrations © Sarah Jennings 2017

The Drum
Text © Becca Heddle 2017
Illustrations © John Solomon 217

A Big Egg for Hen
Text © Juliet Clare Bell 2017
Illustrations © Daron Parton 2017

British Library Cataloguing in Publication Data
Data available

ISBN: 978-0-19-277378-4

10 9 8 7 6 5 4 3

Paper used in the production of this book is a natural, recyclable product made from
wood grown in sustainable forests. The manufacturing process conforms to the
environmental regulations of the country of origin.

Printed and bound in Great Britain by Bell and Bain Ltd, Glasgow

Acknowledgements

Series Editor: Nikki Gamble

How this collection works

This collection offers six funny, action-packed, heart-warming and thought-provoking stories to engage your child and encourage reading progression. The stories are specially written to support and develop your child's early reading skills as they start to use letters and sounds to read simple words, and are fully in line with the phonics your child is learning at school.

How to use this book

Reading should be a shared and enjoyable experience for both you and your child. Pick a time when your child is not distracted by other things, and when they are happy to concentrate for about 10 minutes. Let them choose one or two of the stories for each reading session, so that they don't get too tired.

Read the tips on the next page, as they offer ideas and suggestions for getting the most out of this collection.

Tips for reading the stories together

Step 1 – Look together at the title page for each story before your child starts to read. What does your child think the story will be about? Use clues from the title and picture and talk about what might happen.

Step 2 — Ask your child to read the story out loud. Encourage them to stop and look at the pictures, and talk about what they are reading — either during the reading session, or afterwards. Your child will be able to read most of the words in the story, but if they struggle with a word, remind them to say the sounds in the word from left to right and then blend the sounds together to read the word, e.g. *b-a-ck-p-a-ck, backpack*. If they come across a tricky word that they cannot sound out, simply read the word to your child, e.g. *I, the, no*.

Step 3 — When your child has finished reading the story, discuss it together. Then turn to the fun activities at the end. These will help your child think and talk about what they have read.

Contents

OXFORD
UNIVERSITY PRESS

Sam's Backpack

Written by Teresa Heapy

Illustrated by Sarah Horne

Sam has a backpack.

Sam taps in the tent pegs.

tap
tap

Sam has a pan.

Sam has a cup.

It is hot.

Sam has a sun hat.

It is wet.

Sam has an umbrella.

Sam has a backpack.

Talk about it!

What did I cook in my pan?

What happened to my umbrella?

How did I keep dry in the end?

19

Spot the difference

Can you spot three differences between these pictures?

Answers: Sam's umbrella, cup and tail are missing.

Missing letters

Write the missing letters to finish the words!

p__g

p__n

c__p

b__ckp__ck

Bam and Red

Written by Michelle Robinson

Illustrated by Ashley King

Red has a drum.

Bam has a go.

Bang!
Bang! Bang!
Bang!

Rip!
Snap!

Red is cross.

Bam has a tub and a pot.

Bam has a pan.

Bam hits the pan.

Bam pats the pot
and taps the tub.

Red has a go.

Bang! Thud!
Bang!

Talk about it!

What did I use to hit the pan?

How did I feel when Bam broke my drum?

Were we friends in the end?

Match the sounds

Which letter sounds do these things start with?
Match the pictures to the letters.

d

R

t

B

A Bump in the Bed

Written by Narinder Dhami

Illustrated by Feronia Parker-Thomas

Is it a fat rat?

Is it a big frog?

45

Talk about it!

Who told me to go to bed?

Why didn't I jump straight into bed?

Was there really something scary in the bed?

Did I go to bed in the end?

What was the bump?

Draw a line to match the bump with the thing that made it!

The Dragon Balloon

Written by Cheryl Palin

Illustrated by Sarah Jennings

Pip has a balloon.

A big dragon balloon!

55

The balloon bobs up and up.

Can Tom grab it?

Can Ben grab it?

It is fun!

A hen has to run.

Dad picks Pip up.

Talk about it!

How did I feel when I let go of the balloon?

Did the children catch my *balloon* in their net?

What happened when a hen saw my *balloon*?

Balloon maze

Draw a line to help Pip get to her lost balloon.

Who has the balloon?

Untangle the lines to find out who's holding the balloon!

The Drum

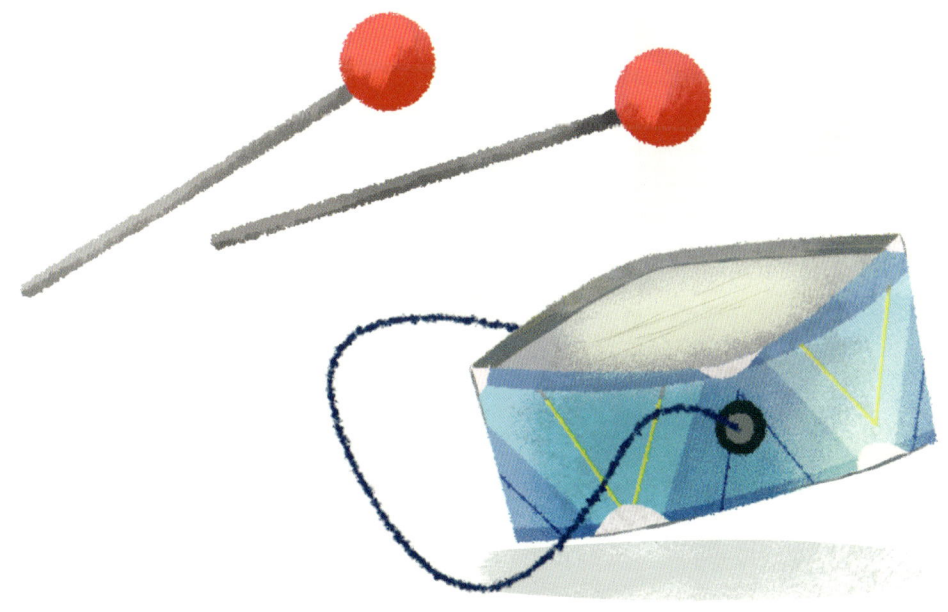

Written by Becca Heddle

Illustrated by John Solomon

I tap the drum on top!

I cannot stop.

I tap a cup.

I hit a tin.

I tap a pot.

I hit a bin.

I hit a log.

I tap a sack.

A paw pops out.

It taps me back!

Talk about it!

Put us in order!

Write numbers 1 to 7 to show the order the girl tapped the different things. The first one has been done for you.

sack ____

cup ____

bin ____

drum **1**

log ____

pot ____

tin ____

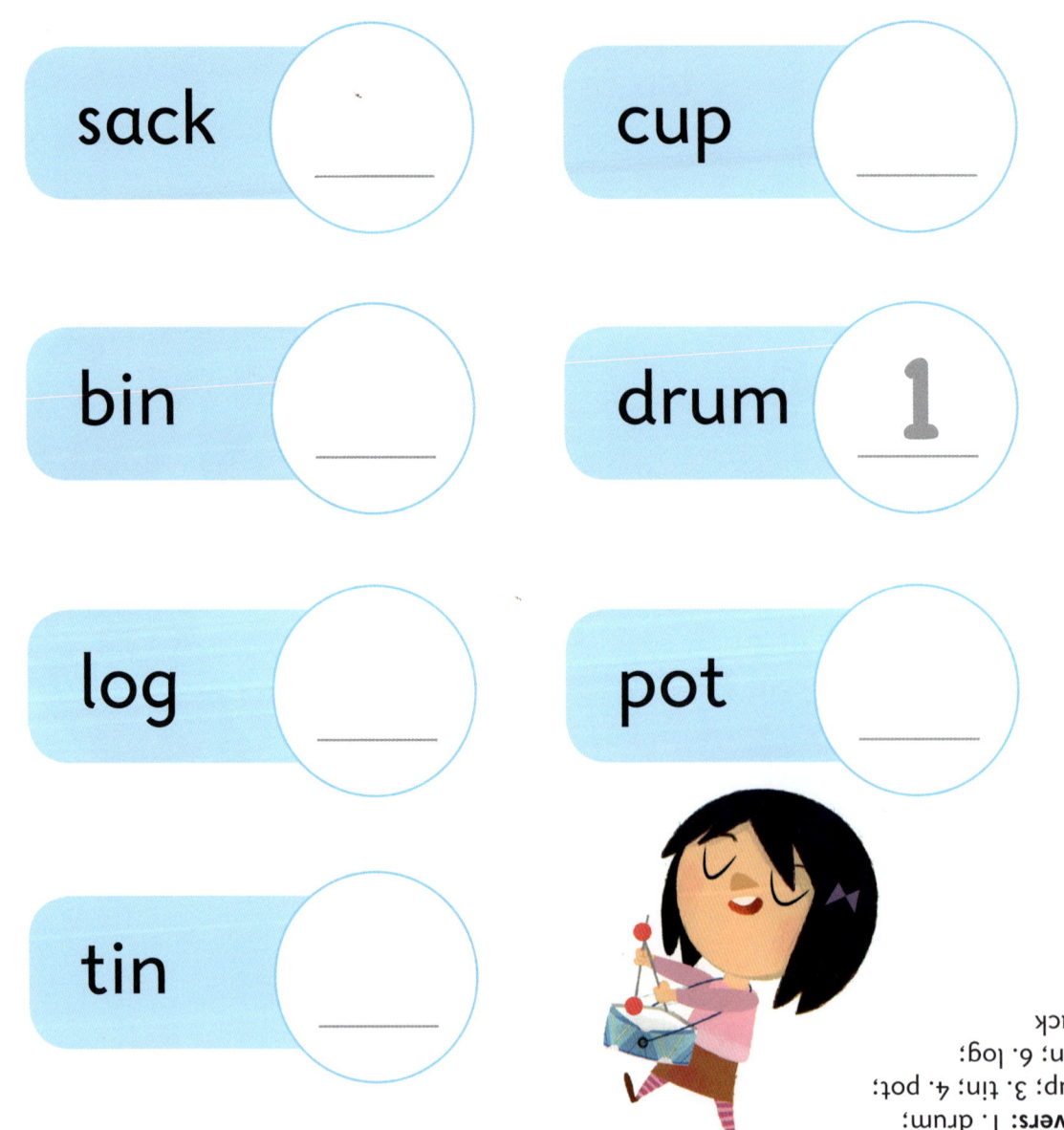

80

A Big Egg for Hen

Written by **Juliet Clare Bell**

Illustrated by **Daron Parton**

Hen has an egg.

84

crack

CRACK!

The egg has a
dinosaur in it!

The dinosaur has a grin.

It is a very big grin.

91

The dinosaur has a mum.

Talk about it!

What was odd about my egg at the start of the story?

How did I know my egg was about to hatch?

What was in the egg?

Match the mum!

Match the dinosaur to its mum.